THE MOTHER TREE

BY CHELSEA FRASER

FOREWORD BY KIMBERLY PHINNEY

vine & shoots

publishing

vine & shoots publishing
For information about vine & shoots publishing,
contact vineandshoots@gmail.com

ISBN: 979-8-9894-664-1-2
Cover design © 2025, Joshua Blankenship.
Layout design by Lauren Anderson, Skrade Design

Disclaimer: this book is the creative product of the author and for
leisure purposes only.

TO MY FAMILY

my mother and me, both daughters of trouble, mothers of hope
the men who grew me: my incomparable Iain and our sons, Kade, Callum, and Duncan
and my father, sister, and grandparents for being my forest

CONTENTS

Foreword xi

Preface xv

Tabula Rasa 3

ROOTS

Imago Dei 7

Daughter of Trouble, Mother of Hope 9

Identity 11

The Naming 13

December 17 15

Large 17

Beyond Grief 19

Momma 21

To Be a Moving Stream 23

a leaf's work 25

Pollinators 27

A Memory: I 29

Providence 31

TRUNK

Maple Me 35

Acquaintance 37

Mountain Spells 39

Waiting Room 41

Khesed 43

Matrescence 45

North Star 49

Topped 51

A Song: I 53

CONTENTS

TRUNK *(Continued)*

Impatience 55

Sums of Sons 57

Dangerous 59

Winter Blooms 61

Anew 63

CROWN

Covering 67

A Family Tree 69

The First Sapling 73

Mangrove Delivery 75

December Child 77

A Song: II 79

Relentless 81

March 11 83

Shelter #5 at Sulphur Springs 85

Ecliptic Paths 87

His Drawings 89

Son at Two 91

Dancing on Air 93

Ars Poetica 95

The Mother Tree 97

CANOPY

Evensong 101

The Arborist 103

Engulfed 105

By the Island Counter 107

Human Dendrology 109

CONTENTS

CANOPY *(Continued)*

Celestial 111

A Meditation on Hope 113

Through a Glass 115

The Olive Tree 117

This, the Forest 119

Covered 121

Acknowledgments 123

Previously Published Work 127

About the Author 129

About the Publisher 131

FOREWORD

The first thing you should know about Chelsea's debut poetry collection, *The Mother Tree*, is that it is like the trunk of a mighty oak tree and the many rings it blooms as it grows from a tiny sapling to the giant of the forest we have come to love—year after year, decade after decade, century after century. It is in these layers where the hidden beauties of life are found: in the surviving of seasons, in the collection of memories, in the stacking of time, in the burst of leaves.

Chelsea's collection is at once a memoir and family portrait, as it exalts, overturns, and examines what it is to be a mother and one part of a moving, living, growing family tree. *The Mother Tree* carries within its roots and branches a verse that sings, grieves, reflects, and connects Chelsea to her children and husband and all of the mothers (and fathers) who came before her.

With her generous extended metaphor of the tree, Chelsea adeptly unpacks what it means to be human in the intimate, familial moments that often go overlooked. The candor, wit, and tenderness of *The Mother Tree* is—at its heart—a collection of Joshua stones that points to God's faithfulness through all of our everyday trials and blessings within family life. Chelsea's verse is a remembering of God's mercy toward the unborn child, the daughters, the wives, and the mothers. It is also an equal testament to God's paternal love, one that surrounds a woman's sacred, life-giving work with the hearth of family—with husbands, fathers, sons, and more.

In a broader sense, *The Mother Tree* is also about the universal human experience of being and becoming. No matter the roles we serve in and the work we are called to do, when embodied, there is a Higher Voice—one that calls us out and beyond our limited capacities toward something far more spacious and rich: the work of growing the human heart and spirit in eternal, self-less love. This love is a love C.S. Lewis referred to as Charity (*Agape*) in his masterwork, *The Four Loves*. Lewis writes this about our "chief aim" in life:

"For the dream of finding our end, the thing we were made for, in a Heaven of purely human love could not be true unless our whole Faith were wrong. We were made for God. Only by being in some respect like Him, only by being a manifestation of His beauty, loving-kindness, wisdom or goodness, has any earthly Beloved excited our love. It is not that we have loved them too much, but that we did not quite understand what we were loving. It is not that we shall be asked to turn from them, so dearly familiar, to a Stranger. When we see the face of God we shall know that we have always known it. He has been party to, has made, sustained and moved moment by moment within, all our earthly experiences of innocent love. All that was true love in them was, even on earth, far more His than ours, and ours only because His."

This love we have is real, but it is through a mirror dimly. It is a foretaste of the Great Love we will come to know in full one day—the *Agape* we strive to know—and that is what makes it a worthy pursuit. This Becoming is a deep and holy work, only made real by the years, the sacrifices, the roots, the trunks, the branches, and the hearty leaves of family life.

This is the story of *The Mother Tree*—the story of Chelsea's life *and ours*. I pray every line rises up to meet you exactly where you are. I pray it holds a mirror up to your soul and calls to mind the polaroids of your family life—so that you might remember the hidden love buried like an acorn deep within the soil of ordinary days. And in that remembering, I pray you might find yourself basking in the shade of your Mother Tree and your Father's Love.

Blessing to you, dear reader.

Kimberly Phinney
English professor,
founder of www.TheWayBack2Ourselves.com,
and author of *Of Wings and Dirt*

Women's Work

| *by Kimberly Phinney*

My little girl couldn't sleep tonight—
my gentle, anxious child.
And though my body hurt so much,
in that bone-aching way of exhaustion,
I summoned my strength
for this midnight shift
of motherhood
I dare not miss.

And I thought to myself,
deep into my watch—
These are the most important stories
I will ever tell.
These are the most important songs
I will ever sing.
These are the most important prayers
I will ever say.
This is the most important work
I will ever do.
To be here for this tender heart.
To bear witness to her needs.
And to tend to them with all myself.

So, let the dishes stack, I say.
Let the poems sit.
Let ambitions cease a while.
Tell the World to wait.
There's nowhere else I rather be
than to be right here with her—
doing this woman's work.

*first published in *Of Wings and Dirt*

PREFACE:
OUR MINGLED ROOTS

"You need to start writing again."

It was almost an audible command. After years of writing poetry, studying literature, reading all the books I could get my hands on, and journaling nearly daily, I had somehow stopped so reflexively that I hadn't even realized.

And, yet, there was so much more to "stopping" than a mere reflex. It took years to get to this place.

I grew up in a family of professional artists. They were graduates from Pratt Institute, Yale Arts, SCAD's MFA Program, and NY's Theological Seminary. They were art professors and community musical theatre performers, directors and actors, church choir singers, as well as musicians, writers and painters and designers. You can see that I have *always* been surrounded by the arts. But I never felt like I was an artist myself. My sister had a pad of paper and a writing implement in her hand for as long as I could remember. Somehow she was an artist, but I wasn't.

And yet, I played the piano since I could sit up safely on the piano bench. I wrote stories, and my sister and I would record "radio dramas" on our cassette player—a modern day Jo March, if I do say so myself. I watched movies over and over, read good books over and over—learning story and character by osmosis. I sang in choirs, played the oboe, and always wrote music at the piano keyboard. And as I grew, so did my creativity.

I remember my introduction to John Donne in ninth grade. His poetry was life-changing. Then, I keenly recall how my introduction to John Milton in tenth grade changed my life—again. I was writing poetry then, too, and quite a lot. And I somehow found my way to an English award when I graduated high school and then an English Literature major in college where (Guess what!) I kept writing. And even after all of this, I never thought of myself as a "creative writer" or even a "writer." It still didn't sink in that I was one of the artists in my family. These behaviors were so invisible to me at the time, that when they fell away, one by one, I didn't even notice.

How could that have happened?

Well, I went to graduate school to study Organizational Communication, where my writing style was considered "fluffy" rather than metaphorical or inventive. So I adapted to the business and academic styles required of me without leaving room for creative writing on the side. This was the first chink in my creative productivity.

Then, I got married to my husband Iain, and all of the rhythms that served me as a single woman were forced to change. My husband and I moved internationally—twice. The move to Canada was planned, but the move back was unexpected. The second move included a separation during which Iain wasn't allowed into the country. Also, in the middle of this move, we found out that we were expecting our first child, and with a complicated pregnancy no less. These were more chinks in my creative expression.

My first son experienced a lot of my trauma secondhand while he was in the womb. God miraculously allowed my husband to be present for his birth and made a way for Iain to stay in the country until his permanent residency paperwork was completed. After some time, I accepted a job in higher education, teaching rhetoric and organizational communication and leadership—living in my analytical brain full time. Again, a chink.

I had a second baby who was born early and needed a stay in the NICU. These first two pregnancies were life-changing and difficult. And they both happened while I was working full-time as a college instructor. Although I loved teaching and helping young adults grow in their capabilities and expertise, it wasn't a forever work for me. Soon, God made me uncomfortable in this vocation before He moved me into an administrative role in higher education. More left brain domination, and even less of a creative life. Yes, another chink, and I was withering.

My third son was born just months before Covid shut down everything, and I was (like many of us) figuring out how to work from home full-time and homeschool and be childcare for the younger ones. It was too much. I loved being a mother to small children, but the juggling act was impossible to bear alone.

My husband is an arborist, so his work schedule during Covid didn't change much, which meant that I was also stay-at-home-mom-ing three boys for the first time and under "unprecedented" circumstances. I began to hit an invisible wall every six weeks or so and just… fell apart. I even started practicing asking for help because of this desperation. But, being a recovering believer in my own self-sufficiency, I was bad at it and wouldn't ask until the need for help was urgent or immediate, which usually meant that no one could come to support me.

That was the first time I heard the Voice. "You're in a pre-crisis," it whispered. A "pre-crisis." You know, the place before a crisis when prevention is still possible. It was a merciful admission, and I knew that the Holy Spirit was leading me to safety. So, I looked for another job, and God gave me one. In the arts.

And finally, the unbinding began. God opened my ears to discern His Spirit's voice more clearly. He opened my hands to do more than I thought that I could. He began a healing work in me that I had grossly underestimated. And one day, while I was sitting at my desk in my new job, I heard the Voice a second time: "You need to start writing again."

So, I set a goal of 30 minutes a week. (Start small, right?) And I began to try. I began to remember how. I began to reconnect to my voice and to write the messages I needed to hear.

That first year, I wrote 17 drafts of poems.

The next year, I wrote over 100.

On the heels of the call to write again was a newer call: "And you need to share it."

I had never submitted work to a literary journal. I never felt my work was good enough or that I had permission to do so. I never even thought about other people reading my writing; in the past, it was a private work. But I began the obedience of writing and sharing (which usually meant submitting, but sometimes meant sharing a poem as it came to mind with a friend in the moment).

I believe God has a ministry for our creative works, and I trust publishing is somehow a part of his plan. And this book? This is also the product of obedience to write and share.

Once I began submitting to literary journals and being accepted, the one catch was that my embodied community rarely knew that I was even a writer (let alone a published one) unless I told them, which made the act feel like it was about me. *Yuck.* I wanted to bring my creative work to life in a way that I could give to my community, and God started pressing this poetry collection on my heart. He started laying a path for it to become real.

Little by little, He brought people into my life to support and encourage this work. He nudged and smiled at me as I took baby steps of obedience, and now we are here together on this page sharing these words printed in a book that rests in your hands.

I imagine you opening this book. You may be a mother yourself. You may just like poetry. The cover might have intrigued you. Welcome. I am grateful for your presence.

Accept this book as a gift of obedience, and (best of all hopes) may this work generate some spark in you that turns into a little flame to warm your hands and share with your own community, a spark to start a refining work where you live and work and play, a light for dark places, a seed that starts a grove of new trees.

Maybe this book could be a mother tree.

"*We cannot insist that the first years of infancy are of supreme importance, and that mothers are not of supreme importance, or that motherhood is a topic of sufficient interest for men, but not of sufficient interest for mothers. Every word that is said about the tremendous importance of trivial nursery habits goes to prove that being a nurse is not trivial. All tends to the return of the simple truth that the private work is the great one and the public work the small. The human house is a paradox, for it is larger inside than out.*"

G. K. CHESTERTON

"*The clearest way to the Universe is through a forest wilderness.*"

JOHN MUIR

Tabula Rasa

Books and books and more books have been written.
More than I can count.
And I somehow must put my words to page.
What is that about?
How can the thoughts of someone—me—be what this page receives?
How can my thoughts be worth a jot?
I could just delete.
Erase.
As if they never were.
Turn backward.
Undo—
but more would spill out of my head
and heart
and mouth
and hand
onto the ready paper.
It receives what it is given without complaint:
Mein Kampf and *Charlotte's Web* alike.
And how can that be?
Is it possible that, like paper,
like the trees before them, and the ground before the trees,
the earth is ready to receive more fullness?
It cannot be too full for what will come.
It waits to receive.

"

For there is hope for a tree,
if it be cut down, that it will sprout again,
and its shoots will not cease.
Though its roots grow old in the earth,
and its stump dies in the soil,
yet at the scent of water it will bud
and put out branches like a young plant.

"

JOB 14:7-9

ROOTS

Roots don't seem very exciting. You can't see them, and they aren't particularly pretty. If you dig a hole of any depth, you're likely to encounter roots.

Roots are the initial growth of any plant from its seed, and tree roots serve trees in four main ways. Roots are a tree's primary anchor, providing structural stability if allowed to grow healthfully and unimpeded. Roots absorb nutrients such as water and minerals necessary for the tree's health and then store and conduct those nutrients up the roots to the trunk, which continues that conduction throughout the tree.

Additionally, roots often coexist with certain fungi, and that relationship is called mycorrhizae (fungus roots). It is this network of roots and fungi that makes communication possible between trees via fungal mycelia.

Roots are the brains of a tree, and they provide strength, information, and nutrition if properly cared for. Roots are the beginning.

Imago Dei

Light begins its endless travel
penetrating the darkness,
revealing the firmament
—and the stars.
Physics is born. Mathematics, also.
Sculpture begins in gasses and atomic fusion
bursting dynamic and whole.
And down below, a joyous brawl
of sea on new shores.
Geology and plate tectonics
etch their lines upon the earth—
a lengthy sketch of edges,
never quite finished, but ever beautiful.

Another word, and Earth bears fruit,
verdant, bountiful, hospitable,
ubiquitous diversity providing habitats
as yet unneeded, still yet valued.
Riches of earth and water and seed
and photosynthesis from sun abounds.

Joined by the sea,
wind begins a harmony
awaiting melodies,
drifting through a memory
in D-flat major, sweet melancholy
holding space for joy.
Biology begun, it also waits: for fullness.
And come the creatures—
avian and chordate,
mammalian and reptilian,
indeed all creeping things
awake with celebration in the world.
And light and dark

and form and shape,
perspective, dimension, time
all meet in symphony to paint
new stories with chemistry.

And Glory, an alchemy beyond all making,
hangs contended, calls it Good—
And molding dirt into mirrored tapestry
bears children from His breath—
a breath not of this new, good world.
A breath untied to matter, animating it.
These labors of creative love abound:
He makes you possible.

And somehow—fearfully—the time wears on.
And somehow—wonderfully—the time is ripe.
And He who wove reality into being
took all of Time to bring about a you—
only one, and very carefully wrought.
His patient Love and gracious Wisdom
molding a masterpiece—
bursting dynamic, and whole.

Daughter of Trouble, Mother of Hope

Worth more than the price of ignominy,
I was allowed to live. She lost her shine
for maternal glow, a less bright substance
of wholeness, broken to be remade
by the birth of a daughter: me.

Her smile was wide as a cradle;
Her eyes were as kind as milk.
Her strength grew more brittle,
yet able. She encircled our hearts
with her love. Then grew the weight
of loneliness: lost among friends,
family veiled from seeing,
or young and myopic, their own
weights pulling the atmospheric force
of a relational vacuum—where was compassion?

I was allowed to live—and the lifeforce
whose gravity pulled me to myself
was crushed in the vacuum of space.
Crushed, but not destroyed—
the pressure forged a star.

Identity

We do not name ourselves.
Love whispers over us its Hopes,
linking to our roots
and shining light
on branches yet to be—
our names shape the sapling leaves
and moulder in the bark
our very being.
We do not name ourselves:
We become our names.

The Naming

| *for Mom and Dad*

You unrolled a map and found me
in the East Side of London
just north of the Thames.
My name spoke to you
through the Old English chalk wharf
to bring a sea-bright child
out of troubled seas in to shore.
Yellow strands encircling blue
reflections of the North Sea
winding into the soul of me.
Ancient paths route rivers for being,
growing place anew inside of Now.
I was, from the depth of time,
enrooted in the chalky wharf
and the sounds of the sea,
carried deep into land
for kings and queens
at Chelsea.

December 17

Thirty-three degrees is pretty cold
for a Southern girl,
but the mountains warm me
somewhere deep where roots are made.

My fingers chill fastest,
but I don't need them here
for walking or to see.
They're quite content
stuffed into a pocket
or muffled by mittens.

Do you think God's favorite colors
are green and gray?
Life and shade, deep and cool,
Winter's Day.

I should keep walking.
This pause for thought
has welcomed the wind.
But if I bury my thoughts
in a December burrow,
the lee will shield them warm.

It's pretty—cold and clear.
Gray and shrouded,
like God's cloud that guided
Israel to the sea.

Maybe somewhere there's a keep
where I could hole up, warming
my fingers to write these thoughts
rooting into my heart—the mountains' songs
and the wind's guiding

and the gray's covering.

Do you think God has a favorite
of His colors?
Or does His delight extend, infinite
for all the good He makes?

To even the cold. Even to me.

Large

5 feet 9 inches.
Size large.
Resonant vocalizing
Large, too.
Thoughts myriad
and often
Large.
Capacity?
Large.

But if you need less
then I will shrink
and fade
like a shadow,
Large,
but without substance—
falling behind.

And in that flattening,
I recognize wrong.

My dimensions were established
when there were none.
My vapor life
creating atmosphere for more.

All of a mountain
lends its Large to homes,
to perspective,
to beauties hulking invisible
until you embrace their climb.

My largeness is needed.

Can I un-shrink
the way a shadow might?
Embodied substance
standing into itself
Large.

Beyond Grief

Grief lies heavily on my heart,
a canker in a fallen branch.
—Have I been felled?
Am I laying, untethered from the earth,
awaiting Time's certain passing
and Newton's second law—

The gall gnaws internally,
incessantly. Fungal matter
disintegrating my might-have-beens.
I cannot make what I most desire:
Beauty. Verdant cathedral
made of bough and leaf

and joy, facing outward to serve—
but the blight of my own limitations
ties me to this place
where moth and rust doth corrupt
and worms break through and steal—
where I fear I will not rise.

All this decay—spalting, wilt,
the invasion of insects and rot—
sprouts mushrooms, moss, and lichen
in my new roots. Must I die here?
The rot rests heavily, facing inward,
eating away my fallen wood.

Is grief, like all decay, growing new
in me? Providing, wasteless, for its place
in the earth—for the fiddleheads
and for the ground—a richer home,
a better future, a purer dream?
Grief, do you dare bear gifts?

Momma

She sought life,
but all roads led to death.
So she sought death,
and Life pursued her.

She sought love—
deep buried under pain.
So she sought on,
unearthing home.

She sought us
through the haze of years and doubt.
She showed us how to seek
and how to find.

She sought truth
when all her mind was false.
And Truth sought her
without relenting.

Life pursued her
without relenting—
showing how to find
Home.

To Be a Moving Stream

To meander, shallow and babbling,
fall suddenly, deepening slightly,
widening toward stillness,
reaching for quiet,
met by dappled sun and dragonflies,
turning again, meandering
forward—
to be a moving stream.

To flow, clear and clearing
through a watershed of green
and out again—
destined to run through spigots
and showerheads, in glasses
and garden hoses
in service—
but always through the clearing first,

a moving stream receiving stars
and wanderers and searching roots
along with stone and silt,
its ever-changing windings
down and out
and through
to reach—what end?

No. Only to go.

Only to be a moving stream.

a leaf's work

| *for e. e. cummings*

a single reach
arching away
alone
toward the sun.
never arriving, yet
reaching still—
indomitable.
receiving light, and
transforming it:
Life.
it may not see
its company's
shared reaching,
shared growth.
Green lingers
arching less
as its work
reaches again,
an ebullient encore,
blazing red
or orange,
yellowing with age
to arch away
gently,
alone
toward the ground.
at last arriving
with its company
in success
and rest.

Pollinators

The lavender is thick with bees—
bees abuzz on buoyant shoots,
grasping purple baubles briefly
as they sip to heal the Earth
and feed their young.

What joy it brings to see
my lavender so thick with bees.

A Memory: I

| *for my sister*

I remember two little girls in the house,
in the room near the back,
holding tight while the world whirled,
willing joy to reign inside the little house
that fought with darkness.

Do you remember?

Or did we ever lay in the grass,
staring up at the sky?
Blue with white
tutus shifting on the wind,
undulating from tight spins
to leap upward?
Riding the currents of the atmosphere
from their utmost edge
right down to earth
to make the branches sway,
the leaves shuffle,
the flowers dab with every bee's jeté,
the blades of grass shaking stiffly—

and our hair (unafraid of flight)
spinning cirque du soleil?

Providence: Two Ways

The way it curves to a point
Before bending back,
Crouching to rise,
Again retreating
For another leap
—short steps in
A connecting line,
Continually
Sashaying out
And in and down
And up—dances on the wind.

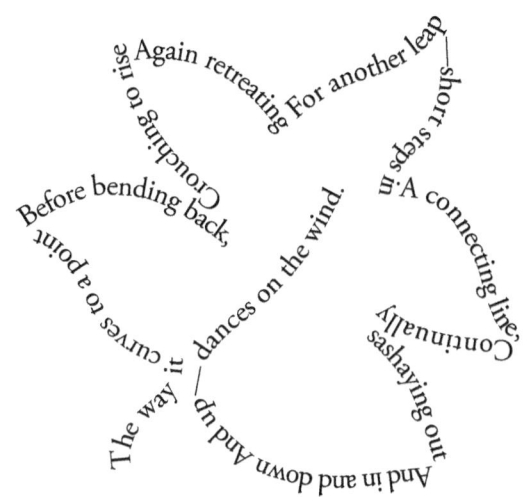

"

That they may be called oaks of righteousness,
the planting of the LORD, that he may
be glorified.

"

ISAIAH 61:3

TRUNK

The trunk is the main stem of the plant. This feels boring. It just stands and waits. But the tree trunk is a surprisingly complex part of the organism. Much like the layers of human skin, tree bark is composed of several layers of distinct and protective tissues.

The strong internal part of the trunk (what we lay people would call "wood") is xylem. And this tree part consists of sapwood and heartwood. It is the xylem that creates growth rings, evidence of an annual production of fresh xylem. Complex circadian processes allow a tree to bear the weight of its continued growth, bend in weather hazards, and even persist in growth if its limbs should be broken or cut off in either pruning or damage.

A trunk is the heart of the tree. Even cut short, it will persist to beat its life in shoots and in defense protocols from both pathogens and predators. And as John Milton once observed, *"They also serve who only stand and wait."*

Maple Me

By cross-hatched trunks
and geometric branches
circling upward,
I raise my heart,
crossed and hatcheted,
its circular beating
bearing up the trunk
of my being—
bearing up the weight
and the fruitfulness
in beautifully broad strength.
I raise my eyes,
surveying all my life
grown here around myself:
the storms and all the sun
that made me, leaf and limb,
to rise in rings that sing of hope
and whirl a green-bough dance
above it all—
I raise myself to height
to stand in fullness,
testifying by each mark, each bend,
each limb that grew toward the light
that bark is proof of the bite;
proof of a resilient life.

Acquaintance

when silence was your company
(around most at least)
and when you hadn't yet met yourself
(your whole self)
you drove me, in an act of kindness
(also known as your Audi)
and we talked right past a turn
(just the once)
but found our way again, and you hugged me
(your future wife)

Mountain Spells

They've always entranced me—
mountains.
Their rise and roll,
their deep quiet
sinking into my heart
like rest.
And even on the day you asked,
the mountains held their trance
until your whisper
woke me—
all of me—
and rising, you rolled a ring onto my finger,
and kissed me deeply
while the mountains watched,
entranced.

Waiting Room

> *"Life is not about not being messy but about being creative with the messes we have."*
> —Curt Thompson

It smells like old
and new.
Old building,
new carpet.
A clash of sense
where I fear I may smell
of old habits
and new flaws—
old pains building
new halls in my life,
clashing senseless
into me where I sit
seeking restoration.

Khesed

The Hebrew word khesed appears frequently in the Bible and describes a mutual, relational, and covenantal love. It is often translated as steadfast love, lovingkindness, everlasting love, loyalty, and mercy.

You fill the spaces in my heart
where doubts would break in,
where the cracks grow at each rain,
the erosion held at bay by a garden
planted by your hand.

You hold the fraying of my mind
and weave the thoughts again,
attuned to the straying threads
in my head, from here and then,
your love tending to the tapestry,
moving faster than the shuttle flies,
faster than even I can see—
you, surest of all ties,
binding my heart.

You make a home for all of me
where friends would wear out—
through warping time your weft
covers and supports me,
shooting threads embracing on repeat—
from end to end—holding on at the seams.

You show the love I often doubt—
that there is space for me—
weathering all my storms,
the thunder and the rain,
with the fortitude of ancient woods,
reminding my heart
that the fullness of the Earth
is too small a comparison
for how wide your love,

the world expanding greater the longer
we go, quarks and quantum material
re-unifying to hold me whole.

Matrescence

*I*mbued with eggs from within her amniotic sac,
*n*o one can deny the birthright of a woman.
*C*onception is her convention.
*O*pening wide to bear pain and life is her magnum opus.
*M*y birthright came in time,
*p*erfection itself in a woman of 25—
*e*ffortless conception.
*T*otal health and home and joy—
*e*xcept

*n*ineteen weeks showed a flaw,
*t*oo small to be noticed—almost.
I was lucky, said the tech.
*N*evermind the hour that had passed
*c*ompleting ultrasounds from every angle
—*o*h, and it's a boy.
*M*y cervical lock was not—locked, that is—
*p*roviding little aid to carry a child long
*e*nough for safety.

*T*ip me over and pour me in—upside down,
*e*xtending feet over heart over head—
*n*eeding others' competencies to cinch shut
*t*he hole (that betrayed me) from opening too soon.
*I*n a surgical suite my birthright almost faltered—
*n*o need—they returned his little head to invisibility,
*c*ircling his exit 18 weeks more. But
*o*n the bed in the triage unit, I didn't know that yet.
*M*y son was not yet safe,

*p*rematurity was still whispered
*e*ven as bedrest became my battleground. Babies
*t*each women to be warriors:
*e*very kick and hold from within a uterine safe,

*n*otched smiles through the discomfort
*t*hat tiny craniums craft within a pelvic girdle,
*i*mmortal joy at life so hard so fast—
*n*o mother-to-be would have it otherwise.
*C*ounting the trials (brings) joy.

*O*perating courageously through the weeks turning
*m*onths, I did what I had to do:
*p*repare for work each morning, daily bear the strains,
*e*njoy the fragile life growing stronger inside (me).
*T*rauma has a way of callusing, teaching,
*e*xcising childishness,
*n*aming fears—
*t*rust has a way of opening, securing,
*i*nviting strength for the difficulties.

*N*o degree of competence can prepare a woman
*c*ompletely for motherhood
*o*r for pregnancy—despite well-
*m*eaning *What to Expect* and Dr. Bradley—
*p*regnancy changes your chemistry.
*E*very time.
—*T*ake a second stab at that thought—
*E*very. Time.
*N*o amount of "bouncing back" can reclaim

*t*he woman before conception. She is
*i*n the past, a foundation for herself, becoming
*n*ew.
*C*onsider the impossibility of an infant girl
*o*riginating her existence with the substance of
*m*otherhood. A sort of potential energy awaiting catalyst,
*p*otential embryos, potential rebirth of a woman as
*e*ach conception brings her to that horizon—
*t*hat wholeness that will never quite be whole

*(E*ven mothers have a birthright.)
*n*ever traveling in the same place very long
*(T*here is such a thing as a phase.)—
I showed up the morning of my induction,
*n*o dawning light had broken into day,
*c*limbed into a hospital gown
*o*nto another bed. He was safe, and it was time.
*M*y doctor came to check on me, and
*p*aused. He was surprised to tell me

*e*ven then, that I was in labor.
*T*he suture had slipped, and my (incompetent) cervix
*e*agerly opened to release my son to me.
*N*ow was the time for my magnum opus,
*t*o lean into the design of my body from birth,
*i*nitiating new life, birthing my own potential-wielder—
*n*ew beings, we, a mother and son.
*C*ompletely incompetent, both of us, for our new tasks, and
*o*bliviously blissful in the infinite love-bond strengthening our new bodies.

North Star

I didn't know that when I smiled,
the glow would reach through space
and point you home.

Topped

There is a pecan tree
in my neighborhood.
I pass it daily
at least twice.

Its trunk is mighty,
reaching above the roof
of the bungalow
standing behind—

but its limbs—
I ache at them—
reaching stumps
aloft toward the heavens.

Their diameter attests
years of healthy growth,
a no-more canopy for squirrels
and birds to nest and rest.

Once tributary for the earth,
to replenish breath
and nourish soil
and bear fruit—

I mourn when I see it,
trauma worn
from abuse
labeled pruning.

The anger that wells
in the deep within me
connects with such lopping
attempts to "help"—

or to remove nuisance
or to be cost-effective
or to work inept
or just not to care—

I lift aloft my gifts,
nubs as they seem
and pray they,
like that tree,

will sprout anew,
awkward, but alive,
reaching still—
resolutely indefatigable,

forgiving of lesser choices
in the contentment of being—
hope's sure testament
to the Grace first planted.

For the Heavens do reign
over the just and unjust,
onto soil that continues to hold
our roots in its embrace

that the tree and I may reach beyond
our different injuries, and more—
that we may demonstrate
our living, defiant faith.

A Song: I

It was evening. Night was falling.
I was wrestling with my longing
When the sky opened wide
With a flood of water.

It was heavy. It was steady.
I was feeling very ready
For that sky to pour out
On my soul like water.

CHORUS:
Help me stand outside in the rain,
Feeling the touch of the sky on my face,
Looking up with my heart to heaven,
Reaching out my soul for your grace.
And every touch of the sky as it falls
Heals my heart with the love of your care,
Sending water to nourish the Earth,
Sending hope through each drop in the air.
Help me stand.
Help me stand outside in the rain.

There is mercy. There is healing.
There is power, and it's teaming—
Grace like rain, every drop,
and it falls upon you.

Feel the earthsong in the drumbeat
Of the water on the concrete
Singing glory to God
As it falls upon you.

BRIDGE:

And the drops, they fall and drench your yearning,
And the feeling seeps into your soul.
If you stand and wait inside the deluge,
You will soak the blessing through in full.
And they also serve who only stand there,
And they also serve who watch and wait,
And we count it joy when weakness battles,
And we bless the one who sends the rain.

CHORUS:

So help me stand outside in the rain,
Feeling the touch of the sky on my face,
Looking up with my heart to heaven,
Reaching out my soul for your grace.
And every touch of the sky as it falls
Heals my heart with the love of your care,
Sending water to nourish the Earth,
Sending hope through each drop in the air.
Help me stand.
Help me stand outside in the rain.

Impatience

"Your anger does not mean you're a bad parent. In fact, I believe it means the opposite. What I believe it means is that you're a parent who wants really good things for your kids and leans toward anxiety."
–Sissy Goff

It boils without heat,
spewing stench of strife
and squelching safety.
Its weaponized whines
wielded by the weary,
white hot and hopeless.
It burns without touch,
scarring souls and scaring—
stirring wrath.

Its antidote is rest—
quiet, quilted time,
quelling questions,
bequeathing faith,
and love, lingering
luxurious in hope.
Liniment for wounds,
salve for scars,
shield of peace.

Sums of Sons

Don't you think math's grand?
that 1+1 can equal 3—
then 1+1 can equal 4—
then 1+1 can equal 5.
Then again, that isn't math.
That's biology.
And isn't it grand?

Dangerous

We are
at all times—it seems—
half a breath
from danger.

(Trees could fall,
lightning could strike,
men to war,
snakes could bite.)

Fire fell today—
unexpected
as it always is,
and with due cause

(electrics could heat
and then combust
in flames that
rabblerouse).

Yet we are
at all times (it's true)
breath to breath
protected.

(Trees stand long,
lightning misses,
men make peace,
snakes avoid.)

And fire falls
to light our paths
and warm our homes
and stir our souls

(For He is wild,
our Sovereign King—
a consuming fire,
yet for our good.)

We are
at all times
half a breath
from Him.

Winter Blooms

We are not all carnations,
blooming glorious in warm,
bright crimson—
pink dusks kissing petals
blushed romantic.

We some of us are green.
We stand the warmth
and soak it to our bones,
such as they are.
And when the frosts come
(as frosts always do),

we push back warm
Camellias,

winter blooms
to show the shrouded ground
that death is false.

Life's buds
abide.

Anew

"I believe in Christianity as I believe that the sun has risen: not only because I see it, but because by it I see everything else."
–C.S. Lewis

Dawn light shares a hope as thick as time—ray
upon ray flinging faithful warmth like smiles—
stretching moments into pageants of joy
for all within its shower-sprayed mile.
The yellowed haze bears forth its golden crown.
It rests on every hallowed human pate
the truth of faithful Love that makes His own
each one who looks and lives—who stands and waits.
The shining power meets the earth midair
and shimmers paths of sky before unseen—
it reaches into leaf and blade, prepared
to share its love with everything.
     The breadth of moment wields a mighty dawn
     that consecrates anew the heart of man.

> **"**
>
> *He is like a tree planted by streams of water that yields fruit in its season, and its leaf does not wither. In all that he does, he prospers.*
>
> **"**

PSALM 1:3

CROWN

The crown of a tree is composed of upper branches, as well as their leaves and buds. These parts of the tree determine the tree's shape and mirror the roots underground in providing balance for the tree. The crown responds most immediately to the surrounding climate and habitats, even contributing to neighboring trees by providing support to other trees.

It is in the crown that trees "breathe" and reproduce. Trees reproduce through the production of buds, nuts, seeds, and pollen, which precedes leaf growth. Leaves are the lungs of a tree, respiratory faculties receiving carbon dioxide from the air and returning oxygen back. These upper branches also shelter undergrowth, providing shade and cover for new trees and other plants as well as animals.

The crown is the body of the tree. Its shape makes it distinct, and its activity is life-giving to other organisms, as well as to its own species.

Covering

The branches cast shadows
as they reach upward to the light.
Such covering incubates new life
and tempers the indomitable sun,
hides secrets and blurs trails.
These shadows can pace time:
covering a clearing
or sprouting a copse.

Reaching for the light
is done through shadows.
Risk and rest lie within.
Hope remains above.

A Family Tree: Two Ways

My sons:
Duncan was born in 2019.
Callum came the year before.
2014 brought my firstborn, Kade.

2012 made sons possible when Iain married Chelsea.
Those two came to Jay, Nancy,
and James, Diana in 1989 and 90.
1988 and 1986 had united
the Bopps and then the Frasers.

They four had been born themselves
between 1950 and 1970
to James, Dolina
Donald, Ann
James, Joyce
Emery, Marian—
whose lives had sprung
from 1924 to 1945.

Ewen married Rebecca;
Hugh and Morag wed.
Cyril and Amy
and Albert and Estelle
had found their marriages.
Harold was joined to Thelma;
Bill and Mildred made a home.
Emery and Katherine farmed;
Harold and Mary lived in Queens.

The 16 lives and love stories—
16 faithful ones—
more than 100 years of fights and laughter,
family dinners, celebrations, griefs,

different countries, continents, cuisines—

all the wars,

all the joys,

all required

for us.

My sons:

Duncan was born in 2019.

Callum came the year before. 2014 brought my firstborn Kade.

2012 made sons possible   when Iain married Chelsea.

Those two came to Jay, Nancy,   and James, Diana in 1989 and 90.

1988 and 1986 had united   the Bopps and then the Frasers.

They four had been born themselves

between 1950 and 1970

to James, Dolina

Donald, Ann

James, Joyce

Emery, Marian—

whose lives had sprung

from 1924   to 1945.

Ewen married Rebecca;   Hugh and Morag wed.

Cyril and Amy   and Albert and Estelle   had found their marriages.

Harold was joined   to Thelma;   Bill and Mildred   made a home.

ery and Katherine   farmed;   Harold and Mary   lived in Queens.

The 16 lives   and love stories—

16 faithful ones—

more than 100 years of fights   and laughter,

family   dinners,

celebrations,   griefs,

different countries,   continents,

cuisines—

all the wars.

all the joys.

all required

for us.

The First Sapling

Kade Morgan James Fraser was conceived in Toronto, Ontario, and born in Greenville, South Carolina, at 37 weeks.

You were coming before I knew I needed you,
and you were with me through my hardest days.
You began in an urban sprawl and brought me home
through a concrete jungle and south across Appalachia

to the place where oaklings reach for open soil
in which to wind their roots—in which to grow.
And you, too, grew from tumult and change,
steadily safe (and healthy) toward autumn's seed dispersal.

And when you came with a rush and a roar
like a mighty tree in miniature, only thirty minutes had elapsed
from silence to sound. You were coming before I knew,
and you brought me to the edge of the forest

where the light shines clear,
to the open field where the clouds stand high,
to the roots of my newly made mother tree
where the soil feeds strength—to my heart.

You came, a gift and guide—through solitude and darkness—
to lead us out from the treeless place
into the light of a temperate forest, colored orange and red
in the morning of October's first day, the morning of our family's first steps.

Mangrove Delivery

On January 24, 2018, Callum Donald Fraser arrived by induction at
34 weeks after my water broke at 33 weeks. He was in the NICU for 16 days.

I delivered a son in an estuary forest,
towering trees swaying in fierce winds
to receive a stormy birth and a fragile babe.
I cried salt relief at the sound of his yell,
for his lungs were so small, and I could not yet know
if the steroids had strengthened their leaves.
Only 34 weeks in the bole of my womb—
through weighty groans sprung my second seed,
whole, but without his full strength,
needing care from other branches, deeper currents
of knowledge and technique—swaddling him with tendrils—
cords and oxygen—beyond my sight and into the isolette roots
wending him safe from the shores of my body—

I don't know what I need in the needs of my child,
and our needs blur and mesh; my own grow quite wild.

This was foreign soil for my roots to move through,
but it was where he was planted, and I received him.
Sweet, he laid all his hopes on my hardwood strength,
and rested his woody will into me, and my soft swollen bosom,
there needing only the sound of the beat of my heart
that remained next to his. And deep in the soul
our mingled roots shared nourishment,
skin to skin, water to milk, root to root, heart to heart,
salty air and too-bright sun. I never leave him,
and my eager sprout showed the strength of a tidal forest
victoriously climbed from 10 ounces to 12;
his incredible shoot from Cpap to O2;
or the day that he suckled the very first time,
how hard he worked! A mangrove limb

sprung from water and from tears, to grow
a beautiful canopy for both earth and sea.

Twice seven days plus two in the tidal woods eased his entry
into the mantle of the earth, eased his lungs as leaves to soak the air,
left their marks in my wood's knowledge—not his—
prepared his roots to hold through every storm.

December Child

Duncan Iain Fraser was born just shy of 35 weeks and stayed in the NICU 8 days without invasive medical need.

You came like Christmas trees to December,
welcome, warm, and deep green—
bearing early celebration
and festive work.
Healthy, hale.
Home
after a time
of preparation—
the work of Christmas.
A preparation for the incarnate One,
Evergreen; another babe to celebrate midwinter.

A Song: II

As a seed becomes a sapling,
Sapling turns to tree,
And each small root grows into bedrock
—if reluctantly.

So Your love becomes enrooted
In the bedrock of my heart.

Slowly,
Slowly,
Slowly strong.

And as a stream becomes a river,
River leads to sea.
And every drop finds home in ocean
—if eventually.

So Your mercy pours a shower
On the desert of my heart.

Slowly,
Slowly,
Slowly strong.

But my faith is small and feeble.
Is it there at all?
Still You find me in the silence
And give my voice a song:

To know You ever deeper
And to seek You all my days.

Even if slowly,
Slowly,
Slowly strong.

Boundless

Tumbling toward dramatic,
    the waters fall free.
Their racing heaves an ocean
    down a mountainous ravine.
And once
    arrived at
        bottom,
        they crash
            and bounce
            and whirl,
                and cry in splashes joyful,

                        "Again!

                            Again!

                                Again!"

March 11

It's green now.
The right berth of the wood shed
is nearly empty.
Warmth is waxing larger week to week,
buds shedding sneezes
that will be flowers
or trees.

My toddler helps "gard" with me:
mini-garden guard,
shovel in hand
bouncing toward my bent frame,
reaching into earth to purge the weeds—
his eager play shovel working with the shimmers of Eden.

Lord, make me that green again.

Shelter #5 at Sulphur Springs

Cardinals, wrens, finches, all
calling to the morning—
fellowship of treesongs,
dew—hops between earth and sky
bourne on whistle calls—

dappled, lilting day awaking
new, and just like yesterday—
both fresh and ordinary,

babblings through the night
looping harmonies for flying soprano libretto—
awakening ancient rhythms
with each daybreak's aviary improvisations.

I need this music of the earth
to wind into my bones, rooting me
on life-wings—upward to perch

listening to the water and the woods
and the hope and the health
sounding airdrop to feather
to bark to bladed grass—
a crescendo of life swells from the ground

holy noises symphonic
swaying to the earth's trochaic heartbeat
toward Heaven—and beyond.

Ecliptic Paths

Eldest forging forward into the unknown
of elementary and existential air,
moving fast, a summer constellation,
from second to third grade, illiterate to author.
And on it goes, this growth and speed
through the planetary changes of a boy
becoming man—forging a way through blood
and boredom, both. His mother sees this path:
firstborn herself, forging forward with unknown
futures, certain fears, and faith to follow.
Her blood and boredom both fueling the fire
to shield and guide her eldest, first of three,
through their unknown growings toward manhood
and toward their Father's heart.

His Drawings

It isn't glamorous
or comfortable,
but it's what he draws.
Every time.
It's what he draws:
us, perched on the bed's edge—
the pictures of his parents' love.
The calm presence
remaining until sleep,
through cricks in the neck
and reduced circulation
from contorted hugs
or rubbing his back.
And it's what he draws—

the twists and bends of his parents' hearts
bear room in their rest,
making way for little homes,
attending to the beds
that tuck-in unwillingly for sleep.
This ordinary gift of presence:
he draws that he is loved.

Son at Two

Somewhere a boy with golden curls
is playing in a field.
His eyes are blue;
his cheeks are flushed;
his feet are never still.
Exploring is his favorite task,
and everywhere he goes
he brightens, as does sunshine,
the clover at his toes.

Dancing on Air

Butter sizzles, smelling salty and warm,
ready for a vegetable to become ensconced
in liquid happiness. Playful shrieks run up and down the hall,
enamored with imagined battles
seizing their minds, becoming alive.

Familiar music lays beneath the ordinary,
animating my feet and turning my body weightless
and lithe, despite the soft rolls around my belly,
less limber than willing, yet shameless
as a spatula joins my movements,
conducting the chaotic symphony of brothers and cooking,
side-by-side play of mother and sons,
each sharing the blessing of a full heart,
a contented home, toothsome dinners.
Lightsaber laughter ricochets to catch
us mid-step and twirl us again.

The air is full—and transparent—
and yet we breathe its life and inhale provision, effortless.
Vegetables soften willingly,
ready to deliver themselves for our nourishment,
as I once did—swaying through the pain to deliver joy,
three times over, and infinite.

How these evening passages provide us riches, I wonder at,
even as I smile, overflowing
anticipation arriving to a table
where all our loves converge to share each other.
This dance allows us frequent practice
for the even fuller air beyond the veil.

Ars Poetica

To sit
and to provide
shade or food,
rest or inspiration.

To be
deepening
and expanding
still.
Rooted in the ever-moving earth,

to sway,
to flourish,
to cast off—
to Home.

To sit
or stand
and wait
with outstretched arms,
branching
everywhere
all ways,

for service,
for being,
and for Glory.

The Mother Tree

She bears offspring and hopes
Provision, protection for her saplings:
Her roots, her company, her shade—

Young roots, entwine, mingle
With the aged depths, securing your foundation
In subterranean community.

Share the deep-breathed molecules,
Gravity-pulled into the nursery of your kin,
Sprawling earth-wide and homeward.

Young rings, bequeath your marks
In concentric ripples, time-won,
Patience married with the forest's partnership,

Providing dapple-light for your exaggerated leaves,
Saturating carbon-food, exhaling oxygen,
Expanding with each breath invisibly.
Young reach, exult, and stretch
With the elder branches, ever upward
In worship-postured gaze, repeating

Leaf-claps, wind held captive
Outside the canopy of the mother tree,
Providing for the green-wood practice.

Mother, stand, and wear the strength of prayer
On every whisper or shouting of the sky,
And having done all, stand.

For under and among and deep
Beneath these laden boughs
Grow strength and home and being.

"

...until the Spirit is poured upon us from on high,
and the wilderness becomes a fruitful field,
and the fruitful field is deemed a forest.
Then justice will dwell in the wilderness,
and righteousness abide in the fruitful field.
And the effect of righteousness will be peace,
and the result of righteousness, quietness
and trust forever.

"

ISAIAH 32:15–17

CANOPY

The tree canopy refers to the roof of a grouping of trees, mostly used in forestry. Any tree grouping's collective set of crowns constitutes a canopy.

The canopy is strengthened by the partnership of many individual trees, and together with its undergrowth, provides a habitat all its own. One can climb into a tree and up into a forest canopy, but (with the exception of arborists and some adventurers) this behavior is not typical. So we experience the canopy by looking up from the ground or from flying over its height.

The canopy represents the community of the forest. It collectively interfaces with the surrounding world. It collectively protects itself, its young, and the creatures in its care. It collectively reels when it is harmed, communicates among itself (though primarily underground—remember mycorrhizae?), and—most compelling—stands the test of time to testify that the patterns of life, death, and rebirth are as hopeful and true as the brightest day.

Evensong

Clouds stack themselves on top of nothing,
higher and higher and wider,
flattening against an unseen shelf
above our heads,
rounding upward into the edge of space
until a hidden wind stream
blows them off, away
to dissipate into the breaths we take
or burst—in tears at the beauty of such a world.

Tonight the clouds were roads for Elijah,
orange fire pointed heavenward,
wrapped in forward pillars of grey Presence,
waiting to bring my soul to the throne of God.

The Arborist

My arbor cowboy rides the trees.
He tames the wild branches,
so they quiet. Wind whinnies
wonder at the master in the saddle,
tending the thoroughbred woods.

Engulfed

Hot, threatening feelings
open out of nowhere,
root quickly in the soil of my heart,
and spark fire on my family,
my house—nothing is safe from its reach.
Everything seems consumed.
Standing, still, he burns

unwavering. A ring
around my rage, around
my finger that he gave
and still rings 'round me,
a fire line to quench the fury.
A promise strong to love
through flames. A faithful
husband to love and live

and rebirth a forest.

By the Island Counter

Voices chatter happily,
completing play midst bedtime
preparations. Boys know
better time spent laughing,
cleaning between the ears,
resetting cardiac rhythms
rightly. Rest will come
with peace. Brotherly love
holding our house whole.
Soon they'll be gone,
I'm told. Silence returned,
deep, perhaps unwanted.
It's louder than Metallica
most days. Happier, too.

One day, another bedtime,
men might gather
by an island counter
listening to voices
of the past, echoing
in their homes, reminding
them how to play—
with peace. Brotherly love
full, shared anew,
smiling at the ripples
time wears: Fractals—
weirder than Metallica
most days. More beautiful.

Loose the seconds,
Momentous Now, and hold—
This. This nothing normalcy
is our everything.

Human Dendrology

There is often a pile of logs in my backyard,
annually alternating from a sort of southern tundra
to an abundant playground for my sons—
this year a ship-house.

Every year, we cheer as the logs are delivered
by dump trailer or sometimes
by a knuckle boom truck
large enough to crack our driveway—

That year, we stood in the (particularly) cold morning,
watching a huge metal hand lift logs larger than our beds
from the truck down to our side yard.
The boys shivered in the thrill and chill air.

Those logs lingered alongside our carport.
We played hide and seek in the freezing night once,
with stars and the porch light and lamp post as guides—
hid in and around the giant sideways trunks.

Many an afternoon they'd pretend
the logs were ships or bridges or obstacle courses,
and they'd groan when the chainsaw appeared
to begin our preparation for next winter.

The loss of this playground generated another,
even better one, with dozens of sectioned trunks
ready to be scaled and crossed, marked
and labeled sections of a play home or other bearer of men.

I watch these logs come every year with joy.
And I watch them change their purpose over time.
Trees grew over many years, homes for innumerable creatures,
and I, too, groan when they fall away.

But they bring to our yard new life, new games,
renewed work to provide home for our family
into future winters as yet unseen—
they bring, in hunks abundant on my lawn,

bright warmth and strength and childhood reborn—
a cycle of preparation begun out of mind, brought to my home,
begetting family memories and dancing hearths.
Felled, but not forgotten. Full anew.

Celestial

It is always the cold that tips my head
up
searching for the larger stars to make
meaning of my place
shapes in the night sky
hope in the dark.

It is always the cold that stirs my hope
                  warm
by its persistent search for Cassiopeia
returning her glory faithfully
          from the space
          from her strong crown
          from the dark
              which cannot outrun light's reach.

It is always the cold that reminds my heart
again
what the Great Hunter always knows—
that glory reaches
into space
          into me
          into the cold

ever-tipping my head toward the lights,
              Messengers
for the Glory reaching out its arms to make
          peace in this cold
          home of this place
          place of this dark

always.

A Meditation on Hope

Hope, elusive, hangs nevertheless in sight.
It shines removed or nigh relentlessly.
My darkest nights reveal the myriad stars
more readily than the light,
hope drawing nearer, ever, lightyears on—
and still unreachable, it pursues me
through galactic depths and unfathomable time,
from history, perhaps even the Beginning—
nearer to me here in the elusive moment,
fleeing as it arrives, but never gone,
infinite in its searching path,
the evidence of things not seen.
And substantial Hope abides over my journey,
like it once did over another grumbling people
through a wilderness of their unbelief
though Hope was on the ground every morning,
in the lead every step, in the air every night—

How can I believe myself to be unreachable,
pursued through chronos and cosmos,
from, yes, the very Beginning itself—
I do believe. Help my unbelief—
Hope promised as many as the stars—and I among them,
held aloft, alit by Hope, relentless burning
in our hearts, filled with its faithfulness
to chemical vessels of matter who, when filled,
shine, too, adding their elusively present light
to lead others on their way to Hope
as cities on hillsides, stars in deep skies,
trees of righteousness,
smoking flax—
Hope finds them all,
fuels them all,
fills them all,
forever.

Through a Glass

Through my kitchen window
observe the miniature forest out back
starkly set now against a winter's sky—
grey, more often than not, and opaque.
A canvas bare, bereft of color's mark,
but captivating as a Rothko, undulating slate
within a window frame, stark lines little moving,
if at all. From here, the world is still.

Still, here the cacophony of children's voices
drowns the atmosphere, a rainbow
of sensations pours from the fireplace,
the hall, the stovetop nearby. A contrast
stark inside as out. Observe inside my window
the colors of a happy home. Van Gogh himself
could not paint a better masterpiece than this
twinkling, dancing life. From here, the world is alive.

Perhaps we love December because it shows us Truth;
the liminality of winter life walks us straight to God.

The Olive Tree

for my husband

"You make my stiff heart know that I am yours."
–Homer, *The Odyssey*

Twelve years removed, but not our surety,
held within your heart—too strong to fail
despite the monsters lurking in the deeps,
distractions at each threshold of the floor.
I meet your eyes across deep time itself
and hold you in my gaze and in my breath,
unwilling one more rhythm of my heart
to beat without your smile upon my face.

The olive trunk hewn by your skillful arms,
wrought with all force of love to weave a house
of living wood, bole completed by our residence
and forged before the widest storms broke in,
threatening my mind and honing your patience,
hovering near the pieces of my soul plunged cold
within the waters of three births, three babes, three lives
that blossom olive fruit uncrushed despite the press.

You are mountain drives and oak-strong arms,
Odysseus to my Penelope, forging storms
and countless obstacles to return to me
day by day, task by need, interruption by eye-contact.
Over the hills we climb, hand-in-hand,
sharing awe in the world and in our luck
to be ourselves—known, and held in olive trunks,
together to grow entwined, entangled maybe, home.

This, the Forest

| *for Tolkien*

The forest beckons, step within.
Touch the trunks that rise and shine.
Crunch the moldered leaves enshrined;
breathe our company, dear friend.

Walk among us, wise and wary,
standing time and holding very
fingers, intertwined and buried
mantle-deep. What wealth they carry.

Seek and ye shall find, they call.
Oaken signs of greater halls—
pointing not to the individual
but branching out their company tall.

Never quite alone, our trees—
mycorrhizae accompanies.
Dirt holds riches no one sees—
thank it. Thank it fervently.

From one to many, grown to these
in strengths, which etch on wood and leaves
and meet in solidarity—
this the forest for the trees.

COVERED

In water, in air, in light and in darkness,
In truth, in beauty, in goodness askew,
In love, in hope, in bounty, in fullness,
In struggle, in strength, in mercy anew,
In prayer, in abundance, innumerable griefs,
In promise, in power, in Providence sure,
In victory, glory, in time soon departing,
In peace everlasting, in joy evermore.

ACKNOWLEDGMENTS

This book is dedicated to my family. Especially to my mother, Nancy Bopp, whose faithfulness through years of drought, despair, and darkness has been a beacon of light pointing to Jesus, and whose stalwart creativity through poetry and song has shown me that we are who God has made us to be and that a poetic life is possible. My Dad, Jay Bopp, is a part of my forest, the ecosystem that supports me, and his strength, excellence, and love have inspired and cared for me my whole life. There are not enough thanks for my sister, Hattie Miller, and best friends, Michelle Johnson and Liz Chevalier. You always believe in me, and you don't let me walk through life alone.

And thank you, Iain, my love. It amazes me how much you must believe in me because you don't particularly enjoy or understand poetry. Nevertheless, you have always championed me and this work. Thank you for showing me *khesed* love through the many-colored facets of our lives and for inspiring some of my best work—both on the page and off. I love you.

This book is a product of community, and many, many people brought this book out of me. God's call to write and share was followed by God's community: friends who said a word of encouragement across a table and never knew they were seeding this project, friends who read my work and championed me. This book is a forest unto itself of people who sheltered and strengthened and grew along with it. I am so grateful. In particular, thank you, Emma Stephens for respecting me as a poet and helping me see that this book could exist, Bethany Davis for encouraging me to fly, Michelle Grover for providing a runway from which to takeoff, and to Kimberly Phinney for contributing her expertise and soul to the strengthening of this Mother Tree. Thank you, Scott Laumann, for believing it was worth it to make this book beautiful. Thanks to Joshua Blankenship for your incredible partnership in turning my aesthetic ideas into even better realities and to Lauren Anderson for truly making the poems shine on the page.

Thanks to Lib Ramos for encouraging another maker to get her work into the world, and thanks to Michelle Radford and Luke Cleland for reminding me that I should do what God wants me to do. Period. I have to thank my friend, Dr. Wesley VanderLugt, for encouraging me years ago to submit my work and for continuing to support me as a writer.

Thanks to my early readers and supporters as I figured out how to bring this book to life.

And thank you for reading. The spine of this book is a memoir, an ebenezer of God's work throughout my life. I hope you saw beyond whatever I brought to the page and into God's work in your own life, building your identity exactly as He intends, wrestling with your own insecurities and past difficulties, and finding encouragement that there is a sun beyond the current clouds and a future beyond the present uncertainty. And I pray that the work God has for these lines serves to point to Him and not to me. May we all ever be pursuing His beauty.

SOLI DEO GLORIA.

PREVIOUSLY PUBLISHED WORK

Maple Me
The Way Back to Ourselves Literary Journal

Waiting Room
The Way Back to Ourselves Literary Journal

Winter Blooms
Ekstasis Magazine

Shelter #5 at Sulphur Springs
The Way Back to Ourselves Literary Journal

The Mother Tree
The Way Back to Ourselves Literary Journal

Evensong
Vessels of Light Literary Journal

The Olive Tree
Persephone Literary Magazine

ABOUT THE AUTHOR

Chelsea Fraser is a wife, mother, poet, musician, and arts administrator. She believes that the world and our lived experience are art and that we were made to participate in making beauty. Chelsea holds a B.A. in English Literature and an M.A. in Organizational Communication. She runs FPC Arts, a ministry that uses the arts to unlock and empower the full potential of who God has made each of us to be. She has been published in *Ekstasis Magazine, The Dewdrop, Vessels of Light Journal, Persephone Literary Magazine,* and *The Way Back to Ourselves Literary Journal* and is being published in an anthology titled, *Dear Jesus: Love Letters to the One Who Loved Us First.* You can learn more about her at chelseafraserwrites.com

Chelsea lives with her beloved husband, Iain, and their three boys in Greenville, SC.

ABOUT THE PUBLISHER

vine & shoots

publishing

At the intersection of biblical literacy and literary hospitality, vine & shoots publishing is a spiritual culture care initiative dedicated to creating a viable publishing path for emerging literary voices of Christian women and youth. For information regarding individualized writing coaching and/or publishing services, contact Michelle Grover at vineandshoots@gmail.com and follow @vineandshootspublishing on Instagram.

www.ingramcontent.com/pod-product-compliance
Lightning Source LLC
Chambersburg PA
CBHW051627120626
46551CB00014B/1972

* 9 7 9 8 9 8 9 4 6 6 4 1 2 *